Beginners guide to
MAGIC

Written by Rosy Border
Illustrated by Mimi Everett

Henderson
Woodbridge, England *Publishing*

GETTING YOUR ACT TOGETHER

There is no such thing as instant magic. Would you expect to buy a guitar today and give a recital tomorrow? (You would? You and your audience are in for a big disappointment!).You will have to put in a lot of practise before your magic is good enough to show to anyone.

Don't try to do too much at once. Choose one trick from this book and practise it until you can do it smoothly and confidently every time. A good trick to start with is the Paper Tree on page 5 or the Walking Through the Postcard trick on page 7. These tricks are quite easy to learn and use materials which are cheap and easily available.

When you have perfected one trick, move on to another, and so on. You can then think about putting an act together. Never, ever perform a trick in public until you have got it exactly right.

Think of your act from the audience's point of view. Choose tricks you think they will like, and try to show them a variety of different tricks. Most audiences would get rather restless if you showed them an entire act composed of nothing but card tricks. Plan your programme carefully.

Make sure you can move smoothly from one trick to the next. This means having all your equipment laid out ready and knowing exactly where to pick it up from. Nothing looks worse than a five-second gap while you look around for the props for your next trick. A smooth, error-free performance will do wonders for your reputation.

Get a friend to time each trick, so that you know just how long your act will last. Then you can start either organising background music or working out your "patter" — the jokes and stories you use to string your tricks together.

Music or patter? It's up to you. It is also a matter of personality. If you are a cheerful, bubbly sort of person you will probably enjoy entertaining your audience with patter as you perform your tricks. If you are quieter and shyer by nature there is nothing wrong with working in silence or to background music.

You have only to watch professional magicians to realise how different their presentation can be. Some magicians work in complete silence and let their graceful tricks speak for themselves. Some magicians have music playing in the background. Many very popular performers owe their popularity in some measure to their slick line in patter. We have suggested patter for many of our tricks, but of course you may think up some for yourself. Or you may think of a gimmick of your own. The famous Chinese magician Chung Ling Soo (whose real name was actually William Robinson) used to talk "Chinese" all through his act. Does that give you any ideas?

We are all very conscious nowadays of the magic of science. You might try dressing up in a white coat like a scientist, and presenting your tricks as "the latest scientific development"!

Finally, here are two important Dos and two equally important Don'ts:

DO smile, speak clearly and confidently and look as if you are enjoying yourself. Audiences want to be entertained! Unless you look as if you are having fun, they won't be able to enjoy themselves either.

DO make sure you and your props are clean, tidy and in perfect condition. Real magicians take great care of their props. They also wash their hands before handling their props. Apart from the fact that nobody likes watching a magician with dirty fingernails, your props will last much longer if you always handle them with clean hands.

DON'T repeat a trick, however much your audience beg you to "Do it again". Politely refuse, or perform another trick instead.

DON'T tell anyone, not even your Mum, your Aunt Edie or your very best friend, how you do your tricks. A secret isn't a secret if you tell, and magic is meant to be mysterious.

> **You need:** 5 sheets of newspaper; a pair of scissors.

Roll the first sheet of newspaper up into a tube (fig 1). Roll until you have about 5 cm left at the end, so you can slide the next sheet of newspaper in and start rolling *that* (fig 2). Do the same with the other sheets of newspaper. You should end up with a fat tube.

1   2   3   4

Now press the tube flat and make a cut in it from the top (fig 3). The cut should be about 15 cm long. Fold the tube flat again with the cuts on the sides. Make a new 15 cm cut in the middle (fig 4).

Now wet your finger, stick your finger down the hole in the top of your tube and press your finger against the inside. Pull up and out, keeping a firm grip on the bottom of the tube with your other hand as you do so (fig 5). Keep pulling and pulling until you have a giant paper tree.

AS you roll and cut, you can tell the audience this story:

Once upon a time there was a man and his dog . . . Poor dog, he had no nose. 'How did he smell?' I hear you asking yourselves. I tell you, he smelt terrible. . . Well, they had to go on a long journey across the trackless wastes of Siberia. Now one important thing about Siberia is the total absence of trees there. Plenty of snow, ice and even rock but not a tree for miles.

Presently the dog was looking a little restless. I wonder if you can guess why? Well, anyway, his master noticed. But, being a very clever man as well as an intrepid explorer, he at once hit on the answer. Taking his copy of the local newspaper and a pair of scissors from his rucksack, he made a wonderful tree. And my word, what a happy dog he had!

OR you can simply say, *"I'm sure you know that paper is made from trees. It takes a whole plantation of trees to make our daily newspapers. They cut down the trees, then they chop the wood into tiny pieces and mash it into pulp . . . Yes, of course you know that newspapers are made out of trees. But I bet this is the first time you've seen a tree made out of newspapers . . . Thank you!"* (Take your bow).

You need: *A postcard; a pair of scissors.*

When you tell your audience that you can walk through an ordinary postcard they will shake their heads in disbelief. But it is in fact ridiculously easy if you follow the instructions carefully.

1. *Fold postcard in half.*
2. *Make six cuts into folded edge approximately 70mm long — see dotted lines.*
3. *Make five cuts into other edge approximately 70mm long — see dotted lines.*
4. *Cut along fold from first to last cut (A-B).*

OF course you may have ideas of your own for patter during this trick but here is a story you can tell while you are cutting your postcard.

"There was once a very clever magician. He performed his magic all over the world, and wowed his audiences with his clever tricks and his witty jokes — until one day he made one joke too many. The king of that country was in the audience and he didn't appreciate our magician's sense of humour one little bit.

"In no time at all the poor chap was locked up in a prison cell. It was damp and it was cold, and it was very, very dark, because the cell had no window and of course the door was locked . . . Well, our magician was very sad and depressed, until he remembered that in his pocket he had a postcard rather like this one" (show your postcard), "and his trusty scissors" (hold them up). "He set to work" (snip as you say this). "He snipped like this, and like that, and along the middle like this — and in no time at all he had a good-sized window. Light flooded in. Then our magician thought, 'I wonder if I can climb through it'" (step through as you say this) — "and hey presto! he was out in the fresh air. Wasn't he clever?"

THE INCREDIBLE
SQUASHABLE GLASS

You need: *A table; A chair; A glass tumbler (practise with plastic); A toy hammer (optional); A coin; A sheet of newspaper.*

This trick depends on attracting the audience's attention away from a secret move. This is called MISDIRECTION.

Sit at the table and put the coin on the table. Put the glass over the coin (fig 1). "Now," you announce, "I am going to make this coin pass through the table. I'm afraid it is still rather shy of performing in public, so I have to give it a little privacy." Wrap the sheet of newspaper around the glass (fig 2).

Speak to the coin: "Are you still there? What do you mean, you don't want to? You're on stage — get on with it!" Make some mystical passes over the glass, then pick it up through the newspaper. Of course the coin is still there. Look very surprised and cross. "This is no good — let's try again." Make some more mystical passes, then lift the glass. Once again, the coin is still there. While everyone is staring at the coin, slide the glass out of the newspaper and let it drop onto your lap (fig 3).

Say: "Oh, well, I'll have one more try." You will find that the paper keeps the shape of the glass and nobody will know there isn't a glass inside. Lift the glass again. Once again, the coin is still there. Say: "Well, you can't win 'em all. Maybe it would be easier if I made the glass pass through the table instead. Concentrate, everyone — this isn't an easy trick and this glass is one of a set of six that Mum got for a wedding present . . ."

Now crush the paper down on the table top or hammer it down with the top hammer (saying something like "This hurts you more than it hurts me!" (fig 4) — the glass has vanished!

Reach under the table, remove the glass from your lap and show it to the audience as if it had really passed through the table. Say something: "Wow — that was a relief. Mum would never have forgiven me if I'd broken one of her precious glasses."

4

> **You need:** *A volunteer from the audience.*

Say something along the lines of: "I've been building up my strength. And now I reckon I'm pretty strong. In fact I'm going to give you a demonstration right now. May I have a volunteer from the audience, please? Thank you ... You don't mind being made to look puny in public, do you? Good!

"Please place your fists one on top of the other. My word, you look ready to do ten rounds at any moment. But with my amazing magical strength I can make those fists fly apart with just two fingers."

You   Your victim

With your index fingers knock the top fist to the left and the bottom fist to the right — both at the same time. You may have to practise several times before you get both index fingers working together, but if you get it right your victim's fists will fly apart easily.

"Now, to prove that was no mere fluke, I am going to challenge you to do the same to me. Who is willing to pit their strength against my secret, magic power?"

You put your fists together too, but when you do so, put the thumb of your bottom hand inside the fist of the top hand. Your fists will stick together as if with glue while you crack jokes about not eating their spinach.

Your secret grip

> **You need:** A red ball; A blue ball; A blindfold; A volunteer from the audience.

Say to your audience: "I've been learning to read minds ... If anyone would like to know what exam questions we're going to have, I'll do my best to oblige ... Mind you, I can't help you with the answers ... Allow me to give you this simple demonstration of my amazing power. I have here a red ball and a blue ball." Turn to your victim and place a ball in each hand. Make sure you remember which hand is holding which ball. "I am going to ask you to blindfold me very thoroughly. When you are satisfied that I cannot possibly see you, will you kindly hold one of these balls against your forehead and concentrate very hard on its colour. Thank you ... Now will the rest of you please count out loud, very slowly from one to ten? On the count of ten, please lower your hand."

When they have done all this, whip off your blindfold. Look carefully at your victim's hands, the pale hand will be the one that your victim has been holding up. You can then announce dramatically, "It was the (red) ball!" and take a bow.

You see, the blood flows downwards from that hand, while the other hand remains its normal colour.

Practise this several times with your own hands before you try this trick in public.

You need: *An envelope with a piece of paper on which you have previously written the name of a pop star; Pencil and several similar pieces of paper; A box to put the papers in; A magic wand (optional); A volunteer from the audience.*

This is a very impressive trick. The members of the audience call out the names of lots of pop stars. You write down each name on a piece of paper and drop it into the box. You wave your wand over the box, or make a few mysterious magic passes. A volunteer pulls out a piece of paper and reads the name aloud. You then produce your envelope and ask the volunteer to open it. To everyone's astonishment, it is the name he has just read out!

The secret is preparation and a spot of trickery. First of all, make sure the pop star whose name you seal inside your envelope is a well known one. Secondly, when your audience call out their pop stars, you write the same name on every slip — the name of the pop star in the envelope. So no matter which slip comes out of the box, it will always read the name in the envelope. Everyone is baffled and delighted, and you take a well deserved round of applause.

You can make this seem even more dramatic if you produce three envelopes and invite someone to choose one of them. Of course, they all contain the same name anyway!

You need: *A rabbit cut from a piece of felt with eyes and whiskers embroidered on and a little piece of Velcro where the tail should be; A cap (a squashy baseball cap would be ideal) with a little piece of Velcro to hold the rabbit in place; A top hat; A volunteer from the audience; A carrot.*

Traditional magicians often produced a rabbit from a hat. You can do the same.

Come on stage wearing your cap, which of course has the rabbit folded up inside it, stuck with Velcro. Tell your audience that you are now going to produce a rabbit from a hat.

Give your volunteer the top hat. Ask him to examine it thoroughly. Place the top hat on a table and make a few magic passes over it. Of course, nothing happens. Take the carrot out of your pocket. Say: "Of course, my rabbit is still a learner. He needs encouragement. Let's try the carrot."

Of course, nothing happens. Say: "Oh dear, he's obviously popped off somewhere for a nap. Or maybe this just isn't his sort of hat. We always used to practise with my old cap. Let's see if that will be any better." Take off your baseball cap, taking care not to show the rabbit, and put on the top hat. Make a few magical passes and haul out the rabbit. This should get a terrific laugh.

THE SWORD BOX

You need: *A cardboard box just big enough for your assistant to crouch in; 10 bamboo canes (you can buy bundles in garden centres) 30 cm longer than the box; Scissors; Wallpaper and paste; An accomplice small enough to crouch inside the box.*

This is another illusion. You have probably seen it on TV, when the magician used real swords. This version is almost as effective and much cheaper. You can make it very dramatic and colourful by covering your box with bright wallpaper and painting your bamboo canes. It is, of course, a very old trick indeed, but audiences love it.

First prepare the box. Get your accomplice to crouch inside the box. Look at the diagram to see where the canes have to go. Your accomplice helps you to guide the canes through. As you get each cane into position, enlarge the hole with your scissors. When you have a full set of holes, remove the canes and carefully cover the box with left-over wallpaper, paying special attention to the holes (don't lose any!).

Practise several times in private. The secret of this trick is very simple. Your accomplice steps into the box facing the audience. He/she sits down inside the box, but turns sideways on as soon as he/she is out of the audience's view. You know your accomplice is safe — the audience do not!

Now you take the first cane and push it through the centre of the box from front to back. If your accomplice was sitting facing the audience, the cane would go right through. Of course, it passes harmlessly in front . . . And so on, until it seems impossible that anyone could survive in there. Chatter merrily as you insert the swords — or play suitable solemn music — it's up to you!

You now remove all the canes, one by one. Your accomplice turns round again inside the box so as to face the audience, then stands up — to a tremendous ovation.

Do study the diagram carefully. And, if your accomplice is growing rapidly and you do not perform this trick for a month or two, please check that he/she still fits inside the box with the canes in place!

> **You need:** Any bank-note or sheet of paper;
> Two paperclips, each decorated with a strip of
> coloured ribbon (we suggest blue and pink).

Don't ask us how this works, but it always does.
Show the paperclips to the audience. Fold your
note into three (see diagram) and clip the
paperclips on, as shown. Pull the bank note straight,
and the two paperclips will fly off . . . What is so
mysterious about that? Well, when you come to
examine them, the paperclips are joined together!
And you can see they're the same two paperclips,
because their ribbons are still attached.

YOUR "PATTER" FOR THIS TRICK

YOU can of course perform this trick in silence or to
music, but it does give you the chance to tell a story
as you fold your banknote and clip on your
paperclips:

"Once upon a time Peter Paperclip" (hold up the clip
with the blue ribbon) "fell madly in love with Penny
Paperclip," (hold up the paperclip with the pink
ribbon). "Unfortunately they did not see much of
each other, because they both had important and
demanding jobs clipping different ends of a bank-note
together.

"But one day they decided to elope together and get
married. So they rushed off in opposite directions"
(here you pull, as shown in the diagram) "but they
met up together later, and when I next saw them —
they were married!"

THE TURNAROUND CARD

You need: *Three court cards from a pack; A volunteer from the audience.*

No magic act is complete without some card tricks. Here is the simplest trick of all.

You place three court cards (kings/queens/jacks) face upwards in a row. You ask a member of the audience to reverse one of the cards while your back is turned. To everyone's amazement you are able to tell which one.

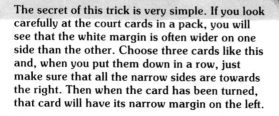

The secret of this trick is very simple. If you look carefully at the court cards in a pack, you will see that the white margin is often wider on one side than the other. Choose three cards like this and, when you put them down in a row, just make sure that all the narrow sides are towards the right. Then when the card has been turned, that card will have its narrow margin on the left.

THE AMAZING
EDUCATED ARM

> **You need:** A volunteer from the audience.

This trick is very effective. It really looks as if your victim's arm is obeying your commands. Stand your victim very close to a wall, with his/her right side next to the wall and his/her right wrist actually touching the wall. Your victim must push outwards as hard as possible with the arm, but not the body, as if trying very hard to push the wall away.

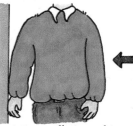

Make sure your victim really is pushing. Say: "Push! Press really hard!" Then ask him/her to step away from the wall and let the arm hang by his/her side. At once say: "Arm up! Float away!" Your victim must not try to stop it; he/she must just relax. To everyone's amazement the arm will rise away from your victim's body. Try it yourself. It is a strange feeling. It is a good idea to try this several times yourself, to see how hard you need to press against the wall, and to experience the floating feeling.

You need: *A wet sponge small enough to conceal in your hand; A volunteer from the audience.*

You could perform this trick before asking your volunteer to help you with one of the other, longer tricks.

Hide the sponge inside your right hand.

Say: "Oh dear, I think there's something wrong with your elbow . . . I'm sure you've heard of water on the knee. Well, unless I am very much mistaken, this is water on the elbow."

As you say this, you grasp the volunteer's right elbow with your right hand. To everyone's amazement (except yours, of course) a stream of water pours out.

Conceal the sponge in your hand.

Squeeze!

THE MAGIC COIN

You need: *A shiny, new silver coin; A pin.*

This is a most mysterious trick. You balance the coin on its edge at the tips of your fingers. You make a few mysterious passes over the coin and it slowly sinks backwards until it lies flat.

The secret, of course, is the pin. You need a bright new coin to make the pin less noticeable. To perform the trick you place the pin on the coin. Pick up both coin and pin with the thumb and forefinger of your left hand. Make sure that your thumb covers the point of the pin.

With a sweeping motion, casually show the coin to the audience — don't let them get too good a look, or someone will spot the pin! As far as they are concerned, you are showing them an ordinary coin.

pin

With your thumb slide the pin across the coin until the head of the pin sticks out about half an inch (1½ cm) over the edge. At the same time stretch out the fingers of your right hand, with the palm of your hand uppermost, and place the coin edge-down across your first and second fingers. Grip the head of the pin tightly between those two fingers — don't let it slip out. Now the coin will stand almost vertical against the pin.

By slightly relaxing your grip with those two fingers, you can make the coin tilt slowly backwards until it rests flat on your fingers. The pin will now be completely hidden between your fingers.

You can now toss the coin into the air with your right hand and catch it in your left. Then you can pass the coin round for inspection, and take a bow.

This trick needs careful preparation. You need someone wearing a shirt in a very special way. First he drapes the shirt over his shoulders. He does not put his arms through the arm holes, but he puts his hands through the cuffs and fastens the buttons. He fastens the top two buttons of the shirt around his neck, and puts on a jacket and tie as if everything were normal. Only you and he know the secret.

1. Drape the shirt over his shoulders.

2. Put his wrist through the opening above the cuff and do up the button.

3. Do up the top two buttons.

On stage, call for a volunteer from the audience
— and make sure your accomplice gets there
first.

Say: "You look a little warm in that shirt — do
let me take it off for you. Of course, we
magicians never do anything the ordinary way. I
am going to take off this gentleman's shirt
without taking off his jacket."

Loosen the knot of the tie and slip the tie over
his head. Undo the top buttons and the cuffs of
his shirt. Then grip the shirt firmly at the neck
and with one smooth, steady movement pull the
shirt right off.

4. Replace his tie
   and jacket.

5. Tug his shirt and
   PULL!

> **You need:** *An ordinary pack of cards; An*
> *accomplice from the audience.*

This is one of the classic card tricks. You will
need to practise the trick really thoroughly
before you try it out in public.

First go through the pack and find the four aces,
laying each one face up on a table as you find it
(fig 1).

Turn the rest of the pack face down and hold it
in your left hand as if you were going to deal the
cards. Look at someone in the audience and ask:
"Which ace is your favourite?"

1

As you do so the audience will look at your face,
at the aces or at the person you have been
speaking to, not at your hands. This means that
you will be able to secretly spread the top three
cards of the pack slightly to the right, stick your
left little finger under the third card and then
square up the pack (fig 2).

2

Pick up the ace which has been chosen. Let us assume it is the Ace of Spades. Place it face up on top of the pack. Place the other three aces, also face up, on top of the ace of spades.

Lift off the top seven cards — you should have four face-up aces and three face-down cards. The break in the pack caused by your little finger makes this very easy to do.

With your left thumb pull the top ace to the left. Say aloud, "Well, here is the Ace of (whatever)," and use the remaining cards in your right hand to flip that ace face down onto the pack (fig 3). Do the same with the next two aces. In your right hand you now have the Ace of Spades and, hidden underneath it, three face-down cards.

3

Drop all these cards (handling them as if they are one) from your right hand on top of the pack in your left. Pick up the Ace of Spades and turn it face down on the top of the pack. As you do say: "And here is your favourite, the Ace of Spades." The audience think the four aces are on top of the pack. You know, however, that in fact there are now three "ordinary" cards between the Ace of Spades and the other three aces.

Deal the top four cards (which everyone thinks are the four aces) face down onto the table (fig 4).

4

Lay them down one by one, not in a pile. Then put three cards down on top of each "ace", making sure that the first three cards (which are in fact the other three aces) go on top of the Ace of Spades (fig 5).

5

You now get your accomplice from the audience to choose one of the four piles. Let the audience think there is a free choice, but secretly indicate to your accomplice which pile to choose — and that pile has to be the one containing the Ace of Spades.

Pick up each of the other piles in turn and reveal each of the three "ordinary" cards. On the fourth card (which the audience believe is an ace) pause dramatically before turning it over to show that it has changed from an ace to an "ordinary" card.

Well — it looks as if all four aces have disappeared. Now point to the "chosen" pile which is still lying face down on the table. Turn the cards from that pile over one by one — they are the four aces (fig 6).

6

THE MAGIC KNOT

This is a very old trick indeed. Uncle Joe used to perform it at Christmas along with the Four Aces trick. We never got tired of it.

> **You need:** *A piece of soft rope at least a metre long.*

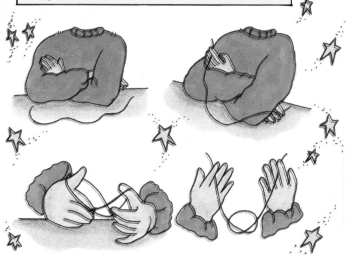

Say to your audience: "I am now going to tie a knot in this rope . . . 'What's so clever about that?' I hear you ask. Well, I am going to tie this knot with my arms folded. That's how clever I am!"

Lay the rope down on a table. Now fold your arms. With your left hand pick up one end of the rope. With your right hand pick up the other end. Now dramatically unfold your arms. Astonishingly, the rope will be knotted!

Practise this trick several times — it takes skill to pick up a piece of rope with your arms folded!

THE AMAZING JUMPING WAND

> **You need:** *Your magic wand; A strong rubber band the same colour as your skin.*

Loop the rubber band on your forefinger.
Push the wand into your fist and onto the rubber band.

As the wand is released it will shoot up into the air as if by magic!

Try to catch the wand and drop the elastic band as you do so.

You could make a joke about your wand: "Of course, this is my new wand. I haven't really got it trained yet. One word from me and it does as it likes . . ." and so on.

Loop the rubber band on your forefinger.

Push the wand into your fist and onto the rubber band.

As the wand is released it will shoot up into the air!

THE MAGIC WAND

Most magicians use a magic wand at some stage in their act. You can make yourself a magic wand with a piece of dowelling about 25 cm long. Any DIY shop will sell or even give you an off-cut of dowelling. Paint the wand black, except for the two ends, which should be white.

You can now use your wand as a prop for your tricks, or you can practise some "wand tricks" such as the one above and the one on the next page.

> **You need:** Your magic wand; A small piece of
> white paper and some glue; A volunteer from the
> audience.

Cut the paper to the same width as one of the
tips of your wand. Roll the paper around the
wand and glue the ends of the paper together.
Make sure this little paper tube will slide
smoothly along the wand.

Ask for a volunteer from the audience. Say:
"This is a terribly boring trick. So boring, in fact,
that I am going to bore a hole right through this
person with my magic wand!"

Get your volunteer to stand facing the front.
Touch the end of the wand against his/her body.
Cover the tip of the wand with your left hand.
Slowly push the paper tube along the wand. To
your audience it looks as though the wand is
being pushed into the person's body. The end of
the wand nearest to you is hidden from the
audience's view by your right arm.

When the wand looks as if it has gone all the
way into the person's body, start pulling your
little cardboard tube back again. As soon as you
reach the end of the wand, grip it tighter so that
the paper tube does not fall off.

Slowly push paper
tube along the wand.
It appears that the
wand is entering your
assistant's body.

The end of the wand is
hidden from the
audience by your right
arm.

This trick and the one after it are based on simple maths, but they baffle everyone just the same.

> **You need:** *A piece of cardboard; Felt tips; Scissors; Ruler.*

Copy this design very carefully onto your card. Cut the card as shown in the diagram. Again, you must be absolutely accurate, or your trick will not work.

Show the complete card (fig 1) to your audience. When they count the diamonds there will be fifty-six. It is quite good fun to get them to count the diamonds aloud.

1

Cut along dotted lines

Pick up the various pieces and wave your hand (or your wand) over them in a mysterious way. Now put them back on the table, but with the two big pieces transposed. So (see fig 2 and 3) the piece marked A has to go on the right, while the piece marked B goes on the left.

Now ask your audience to count the diamonds again. To everyone's amazement there are only fifty-five! Where did the other diamond go?

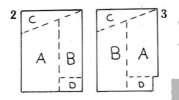

2

3

Count the diamonds — one has disappeared!

WHERE DID THE EXTRA SQUARE COME FROM?

> **You need:** A square of cardboard 200 mm by 200 mm; A ruler; A felt-tip; Scissors.

This is a terrific trick to baffle an audience — and your maths teacher at school!!

First mark out your square into 64 squares — eight 1″ squares per side. Now, using our diagram as a guide, carefully cut up your square into four pieces.

When the pieces are fitted together again, they can form either a square as before (fig 1) or a rectangle (fig 2). Fine. But the area of the rectangle is now 13″ by 5″. Multiply these two together (of course you will get a member of your audience to do this) and you get 65 square inches.

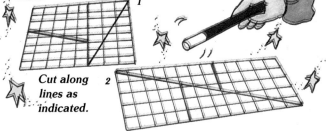

Cut along lines as indicated.

Scratch your head. Say, "Let's recap a little. We started with an 8″ square. And 8 times 8 makes 64 square inches. We cut up the square and put the pieces together a different way. Now we have a rectangle which measures 65 square inches. Where on earth did that extra inch come from?"

YOUR "PATTER" FOR THIS TRICK

A good piece of patter to use here is a story about a dinner lady who used the same trick to make 64 portions of cake serve 65 children!

This is a very popular trick which you may have seen on television. It is very easy, provided you prepare the loops of paper correctly.

> **You need:** Three strips of paper about 2 m long by 8 cm wide — one blue, one green and one red; Scissors; Glue.

Take the blue strip of paper and glue the ends together to make a loop (fig 1).
Take the green strip but before you stick the ends, give one end a half turn (fig 2).
With the red strip, you must give one end a complete turn before sticking the ends (fig 3).

You now have three loops of paper which all look the same except for their colour. But if you cut them down the centre you will find that they behave in completely different ways.

The blue loop will cut into two identical blue rings (fig 1c).

The green loop will cut into two linked rings (fig 2c).

The red loop will become a single loop, twice the size of the original.

To make the trick more fun, you can ask for two volunteers from the audience. Tell them they are going to have a race. Give them each a pair of scissors. Then cut the blue loop yourself, "to show how it's done". Get the audience to cheer the volunteers on. Of course nobody will win because they do not end up with two separate loops — one has two linked loops, the other one large loop . . . Magic!

Before your performance, take your two extra cards. Secretly place the nine of spades on the top of your pack of cards. Put the eight of clubs on the bottom of the pack.

To start the trick, go through the pack and remove the nine of spades and the eight of clubs. Show them to the audience. Say: "I am going to throw all the cards up in the air, and I am hoping that I can catch these two. I haven't done this trick before, so I hope you'll give me plenty of encouragement." Place both the cards in the centre of the pack.

Put at extra nine of spades at top of pack.

Put an extra eight of clubs at bottom of pack.

During your act go through this pack of cards and take out other nine of spades and eight of clubs — show these and replace them in centre of pack . . . then . . .

Say: "One, two, three — go!" and throw all the cards into the air. BUT at the same time tighten your grip on the top and bottom cards. All the cards will be thrown into the air except these two, which were of course the cards you put there so carefully before the show.

throw all the cards into the air!

But at the same time keep a tight grip on the top and bottom cards!

Show the two cards to the audience. Say modestly: "Well, it wasn't easy but I seem to have managed it this time. Thank you so much." And take a bow!

It looks as if you have caught them in mid-air.

THE MAGIC MEMORY

You write the numbers from one to ten on the board. One by one members of the audience call out the names of ten objects which you write on the board against the numbers. You now stand with your back to the board, and yet you are able to call out the correct number for each object, call out the objects in their correct order and as a final feat of memory call out all the objects in reverse order.

There is absolutely no trickery in this demonstration. It is all done by a simple principle which you can use to memorise facts at school or shopping lists for Mum. First you have to learn all the keywords. See our picture. One is a bun, two is a shoe, and so on.

1   Bun   2   Shoe   3   Tree

4   Door   5 Hive   6   Sticks

7   Heaven

                  8   Gate   9   Mine

          10   Hen

Now, as each object is called out, and as you write the name of the object down on the board, you make a picture in your mind of that object with the key word for that number. So if number one is a key, think of a key in a bun. If number two is a matchbox, think of a matchbox balanced on a shoe, and so on. If you can make these mental pictures funny, they will be easier to remember.

When you have written down all ten objects, stand with your back to the board. Then ask the audience to call out any number from one to ten. As soon as the number is called, think of the key word for that number. You will find that the mental picture you made will pop up into your mind as if by magic, and you will be able to say what the object is. Then, when an object is called, think of your mental picture again and you will be able to remember the number too. Finally, run through the list both backwards and forwards, calling out both numbers and objects.

As you get really good at this, try thinking up some key words for the numbers from eleven to twenty and see if you can build up to twenty objects at a time.

Appearing and disappearing tricks are called illusions. Many illusions need very bulky and expensive equipment. This one is practically free. You can beg your boxes from a supermarket and cover them with left over wallpaper or wrapping paper. Be careful when you do this, however, as you have to be able to fold both cartons flat.

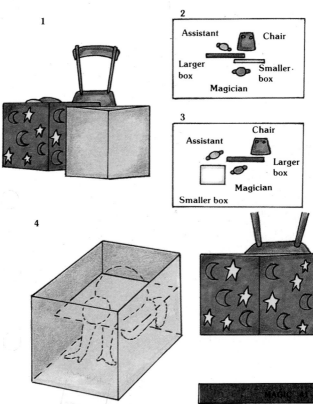

1

2

Assistant   Chair

Larger box   Smaller box

Magician

3

Chair

Assistant

Larger box

Smaller box   Magician

4

This trick needs careful preparation. Carefully cut off both the tops and the bottoms of both boxes, so that they are tubes rather than boxes. Then take the smaller of the two boxes and cut a large flap like a door. The flap must be large enough for your accomplice to crawl through. Fold both boxes flat and lean them against a chair. Put the smaller box, the one with the flap, in front with its flap to the rear. Your confederate has to hide behind the rear box (fig 1 shows a view from the side, fig 2 shows a view from above). Make sure your accomplice cannot be seen by the audience.

To perform the trick, remove the front box and show the audience that it is completely flat. Be careful, when you do this, that you do not let them see the flap!

Now open the box out and place it on the stage. Carefully stand so that your body hides the space between the open box and the flat one which is still leaning on the chair. (Fig 3 shows the view from above, fig 4 the view from the side). Whatever you do, keep your legs together. Why? Well, it is at this point that your accomplice creeps out from behind the flat box to the rear of the opened box. He/she now crawls through the flap and into the opened box.

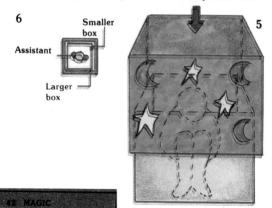

6

Smaller box

Assistant

Larger box

5

You now pick up the second box and open it out to show that it is empty. Place this box over the one standing on the stage (see fig 5 and 6). You can now turn the two boxes around to show all sides, as of course the outer box hides the flap in the inner box. Clap your hands. Your accomplice now jumps up and you both take a bow.

Of course, you can use any patter you like. You can tell the story of a magician whose nephew was missing. The magician hunted high and low, and finally he decided to use a little magic . . . Or you can tell a joke, along the lines of "Last time I tried this trick I got more than I bargained for — instead of my trusty assistant I conjured up a parking warden and he gave me a ticket!"

> **You need:** Two handkerchiefs; A small, very bouncy rubber ball.

Carefully sew the ball between the hankies. Sew round the ball, through both hankies, to keep the ball in place.

At some time during your act, take out your hankerchief to mop your brow, and then throw the hanky to the floor. Of course, to everyone's amazement the hanky will bounce back into your hand again.

Practise several times in private to get this just right.

It is a good idea to do this trick seated at a table. Borrow a coin from a member of the audience and ask them to make a note of the date. Place the coin in front of you, about 5 cm from the edge of the table. Then cover it with the fingers of your right hand and draw the coin quickly towards you, closing your hand as the coin leaves the table. But, instead of picking up the coin, you have to give it a sharp tap with the tips of your fingers and shoot the coin straight up your sleeve.

Now you need to show your acting ability. Pretend to put the coin into your left hand, and close that hand. Make a squeezing movement as if you were rubbing the coin away and at the same time slowly drop your right hand to your side and recover the coin, which will just drop out of your sleeve and into your hand. Slowly and dramatically open your left hand and show your audience that the coin has vanished. You are now able to produce it from the pocket of somebody in the audience. Ask the original owner to check the date — and take a bow.

HEADS OR TAILS

You need to prepare the coin by cutting a notch in its edge so that a tiny point sticks out from it. Nobody must be able to spot the notch without really examining the coin closely. But that little notch makes a lot of difference to the way the coin behaves when you spin it, and enables you to perform this trick.

Borrow a coin and ask the helper to blindfold you. While the blindfolding is going on and the audience are all busy making sure you can't peep, exchange the borrowed coin for your special marked coin. Now spin the marked coin upwards into the air and let it fall on the floor or the table. If it falls with its notched side upwards it will run down with a long, continuous whirring sound which gets fainter and fainter and eventually stops. If the coin falls with its notched side downwards, it will spin itself out much faster and settle down with a sudden flop. Practise this lots of times in private so that you can recognise the two sounds quite easily.

The difference in sound is unlikely to give your game away, but it should be quite enough to enable you to perform this trick successfully every time. Never let anyone guess that you are using your ears to detect which side of the coin is uppermost. Instead, give the audience some patter about your amazing X-ray eyes or your astonishing telepathic powers.